SCHOOLS
in Different Places

Lauren McNiven

Crabtree Publishing Company
www.crabtreebooks.com

MW01527964

Learning About Our GLOBAL COMMUNITY

Author: Lauren McNiven

Publishing plan research and development: Reagan Miller

Notes to educators: Shannon Welbourn

Substantive editor: Crystal Sikkens

Editor: Reagan Miller

Proofreader and indexer: Janine Deschenes

Design: Samara Parent

Photo research: Crystal Sikkens

Production coordinator and prepress technician: Samara Parent

Print coordinator: Margaret Amy Salter

Photographs:

Alamy: © Maurice Savage: pp4 (top), 10; © National Geographic Image Collection: pp4 (bottom), 11 (top); © Bill Bachman: p13; © anthony asael: p16
AP Photo: Paul Sancya: p15; Joel Page: p19
Creative Commons: Brooklyn Free School: p21
Getty: Jonas Gratzer: pp5 (top right), 11 (bottom);
Shutterstock: © LUCARELLI TEMISTOCLE: title page; © velirina: table of contents; © Don Mammoser: pp5 (top left), 8; © Free Wind 2014: pp5 (bottom left), 12; © paul prescott: pp5 (middle right), 20; © SOMRERK KOSOLWITTHAYANANT: p7; © Attila JANDI: p17; © Hung Chung Chih: p18;
Superstock: robertharding: p9All other images by Shutterstock
Wikimedia Commons: public domain: front cover
All other images by Shutterstock

Front cover: Schoolgirls sit in the girls' section of a school in Afghanistan. There is no building, only classes held outdoors in the shade of an orchard.

Title page: Children are shown attending school in South Africa.

Contents page: A schoolgirl is shown in class in Turkmenistan.

Library and Archives Canada Cataloguing in Publication

McNiven, Lauren, author
Schools in different places / Lauren McNiven.

(Learning about our global community)
Includes index.
Issued in print and electronic formats.
ISBN 978-0-7787-2013-3 (bound).--ISBN 978-0-7787-2019-5 (paperback).--
ISBN 978-1-4271-1654-3 (pdf).--ISBN 978-1-4271-1648-2 (html)

1. Schools--Juvenile literature. 2. Education--Juvenile literature.
I. Title.

LB1513.M36 2015   j371   C2015-903953-3
                                       C2015-903954-1

Library of Congress Cataloging-in-Publication Data

Names: McNiven, Lauren.
Title: Schools in different places / Lauren McNiven.
Description: New York : Crabtree Publishing Company, [2016] | Series: Learning about our global community | Includes index.
Identifiers: LCCN 2015029466| ISBN 9780778720133 (reinforced library binding : alk. paper) | ISBN 9780778720195 (pbk. : alk. paper) | ISBN 9781427116543 (electronic pdf : alk. paper) | ISBN 9781427116482 (electronic html : alk. paper)
Subjects: LCSH: Schools--Cross-cultural studies--Juvenile literature. | Education--Cross-cultural studies--Juvenile literature.
Classification: LCC LB1556 .M46 2015 | DDC 371--dc23
LC record available at http://lccn.loc.gov/2015029466

Crabtree Publishing Company

www.crabtreebooks.com   1-800-387-7650

Printed in Canada/032020/EN20200214

Published in Canada
Crabtree Publishing
616 Welland Ave.
St. Catharines, Ontario
L2M 5V6

Published in the United States
Crabtree Publishing
PMB 59051
350 Fifth Avenue, 59th Floor
New York, New York 10118

Published in the United Kingdom
Crabtree Publishing
Maritime House
Basin Road North, Hove
BN41 1WR

Published in Australia
Crabtree Publishing
3 Charles Street
Coburg North
VIC 3058

Contents

Our Global Community

Everyone in the world is connected. We all share the planet Earth. More than seven billion people live in the many countries that make up our planet. Each person belongs to a local **community**. A community is a group of people that live, work, and play in the same area. Together, we all belong to one big community—the global community.

school with rooftop playground, England (page 10)

ARCTIC OCEAN

CANADA

NORTH AMERICA

U.S.A.

NORTH PACIFIC OCEAN

NORTH ATLANTIC OCEAN

CUBA

NICARAGUA

ECUADOR

BRAZIL

SOUTH AMERICA

ARGENTINA

one-room school, Costa Rica (page 11)

Different and alike

Learning more about the people in our global community helps us better understand each other. We can find out the ways in which we are the same, and celebrate the things that make us **unique** or different.

In this book, you will learn all about going to school in different places around the world. Many of these places are shown on the map below.

going to school by cycle rickshaw, India (page 8)

floating schools, Bangladesh (page 11)

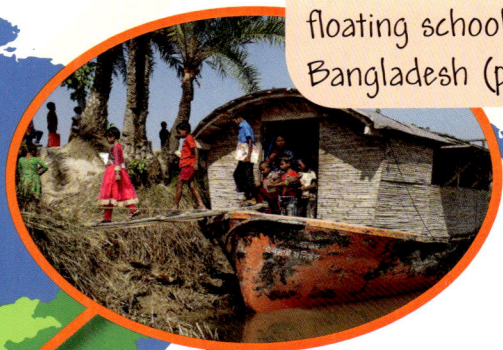

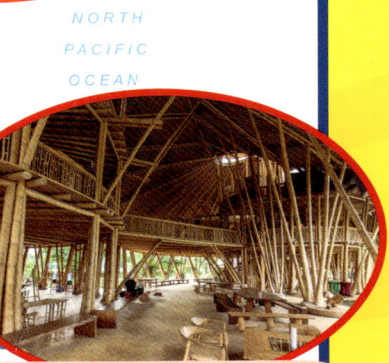

ARCTIC OCEAN

ASIA

EUROPE

FINLAND

UNITED KINGDOM

FRANCE

GREECE

TURKEY

EGYPT

AFRICA

ETHIOPIA

SOMALIA

NEPAL

BANGLADESH

INDIA

CHINA

JAPAN

NORTH PACIFIC OCEAN

VIETNAM

MALAYSIA

INDONESIA

SOUTH ATLANTIC OCEAN

AUSTRALIA

separated classroom, Somalia (page 12)

Green School made of bamboo, Indonesia (page 20)

A Place to Learn

Children all around the world go to school. School is a place to share ideas and learn new things. Children learn to read, write, and do math. They also learn about the different places on Earth and the people, plants, and animals that live there. School also helps students discover what kind of job they would like to have when they get older.

At school, children can learn about people and events from the past.

Life in Medieval Times

Most students use pens or pencils to write down information they learn into notebooks.

Teachers and classrooms

Teachers help students learn new information. In most schools, teachers teach students at different grade levels inside classrooms. Classrooms often include a **blackboard** or a **whiteboard**, maps, books, or computers that teachers use to help students learn.

Getting to School

Depending on where they live, children get to school in different ways. In **urban** communities, such as cities, people live close together. Children in cities often walk or ride their bikes to school because they live closeby.

These children in the city of Delhi, India, are taken to school in a cycle rickshaw. They sit in a cart on the back of the three-wheeled bicycle.

Schools farther away

In **rural** communities, people live farther apart than they do in cities. Children that live in the country usually live far from their schools. They must be driven to school in a car or on a bus, or ride an animal such as a donkey. In some places, schools may be across a river or on an island. Students take boats to get there. Some boats are just like school buses, except they float!

India has many areas with canals, or small waterways. These children in Alappuzha, India, are taking a boat to school.

School Buildings

The area where people live can also affect what their school looks like. Schools in large cities must be big enough to hold a lot of students. They also have to fit in small spaces between other buildings. Some schools may use the roof of the building as a playground if there is not enough space for one next to the school.

This school in London, England, uses the roof for their playground and sports field.

Schools in the country

In some rural communities, there may be only a few students in each grade in a school. In these places, the children may be taught all together in the same room. These schools are called one-room schools. In Bangladesh, some rivers regularly flood onto the land. Children living in these areas go to one-room schools on boats! The boats pick up students from their homes when the land around them is flooded.

Some one-room schools, such as this one in Costa Rica, hold children from different grades. They are all taught together by one teacher.

There can be up to 30 students in a floating school. Most students are in the same grade.

Inside the Classroom

Many school classrooms have a desk and chair for each student to work at. In some schools, such as in Ecuador, two or three students might share one long desk. In many schools, boys and girls usually sit at desks that are mixed throughout the classroom. In some places, boys and girls are separated into different classrooms, or separated within the same classroom.

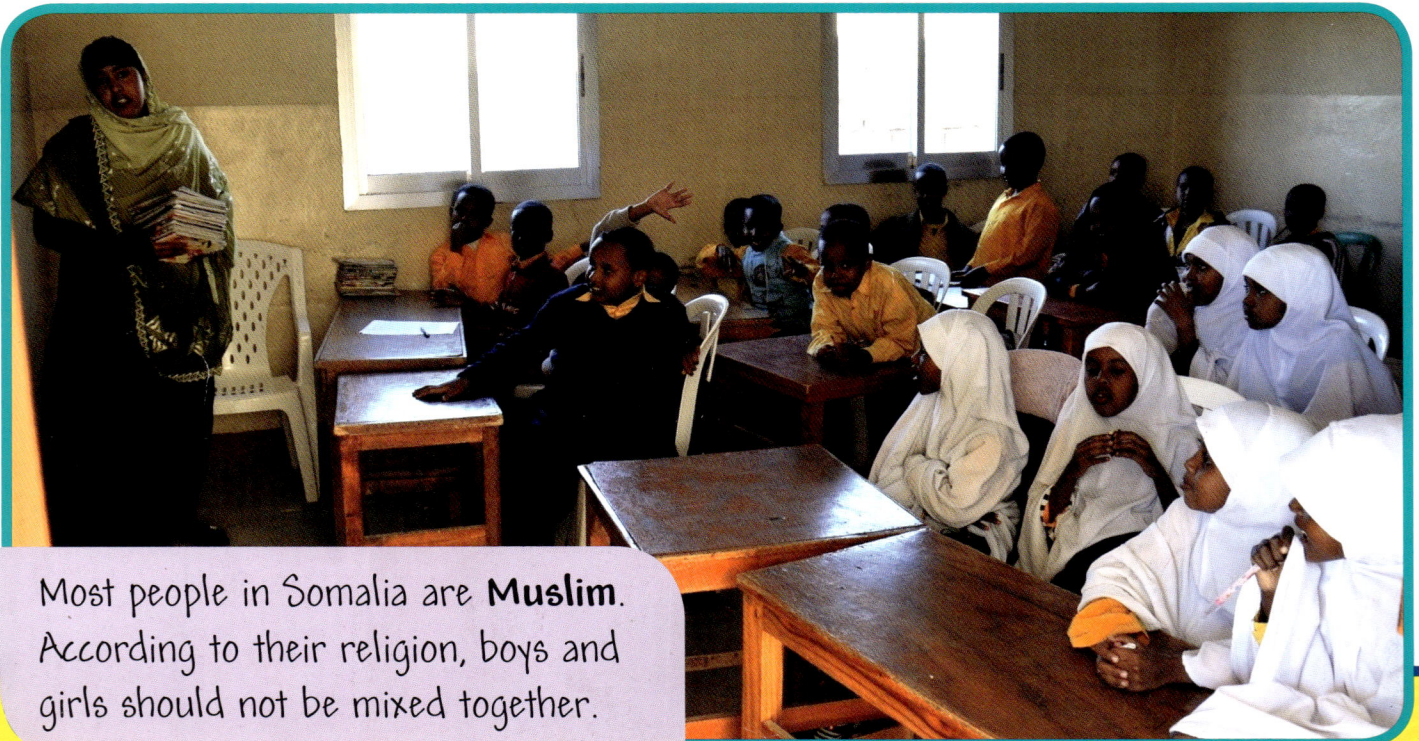

Most people in Somalia are **Muslim**. According to their religion, boys and girls should not be mixed together.

Special classrooms

The number of students in a classroom can be very different from one school to another. Some schools might have only have a few students. Others might have up to 30 students. In Jamaica, there can sometimes be up to 50 children in one classroom. Some children's classrooms are in their own home. These children are **homeschooled**, or taught by a parent at home.

In very rural areas of Australia, known as the Outback, children can learn from home using a program called School of the Air. Students use the Internet to watch lessons being presented by a teacher in a city far away.

Subjects

Students around the world learn similar skills and subjects. Some of the most common subjects taught around the world include math, science, social studies, computers, art, physical education, music, and language. Language classes usually include the main language spoken in the area, as well as one other language.

Hello
Bonjour

In Canada, students learn both English and French. They are the country's two official languages.

This **Jewish** day school in Michigan, USA, combines regular classes with subjects related to Jewish culture and **Judaism**.

Different subjects

In some communities, many people follow the same religion. Schools in these areas sometimes teach the children about the religion. In Japan, many schools include a subject on moral education. Students are taught how to act responsibly, to be kind and respect others, and how to behave properly in public. This subject also includes information on health, safety, and the **environment**.

Rules and Responsibilities

Students in all classrooms need to follow basic rules, such as to listen to the teacher, respect other students, and complete all assignments. In some schools, students are also responsible for keeping the classroom clean. Their jobs may include sweeping the floor, emptying garbage cans, and wiping off the boards.

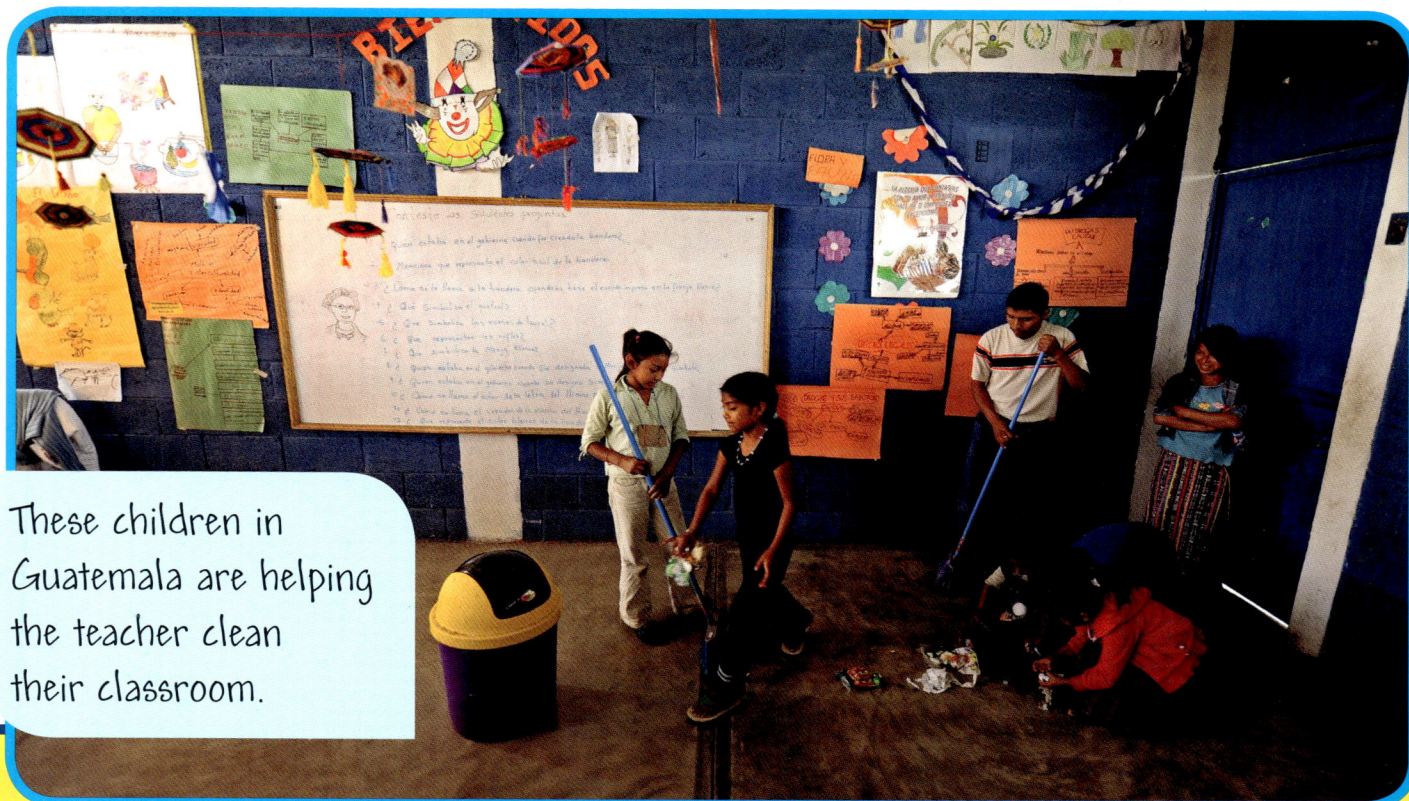

These children in Guatemala are helping the teacher clean their classroom.

In some schools, students must wear the same style of clothing. These students in Cuba are wearing their school uniforms.

Student jobs

In some schools, students are given jobs to help them learn **responsibility**. Certain students might be picked to be the teacher's helper, help organize and put away books in the library, or help other students on the computers. Some classrooms might even have pets. A few students might be responsible for feeding and cleaning up after the pet.

Schedules

In many places, children go to school five days a week. The school day begins in the morning and ends in the middle of the afternoon. Students take short breaks between classes for exercise and lunch. But not all school days are the same around the world. In Bulgaria, most children take turns going to school in **shifts**. Some students go early in the morning until lunchtime, while others go in the afternoon until early evening.

The school day is longer in China. Classes start early in the morning and run until 5 P.M. Often, students must take extra classes on Saturdays.

Breaks from school

Many schools close during summer months because it is too hot to sit in classrooms. In the northern part of Earth, such as in Russia, schools usually close in July and August. In the southern part of Earth, the summer months are December and January. This is when schools close in countries such as Australia and Brazil. In parts of the world where children help out on the family farm, schools often close during planting and harvesting seasons.

Some schools in rural communities in Maine, USA, close for a few weeks so students can help harvest potatoes.

A New School

Some places around the world have come up with creative ways to build schools that are better for the environment. One example is a school in Bali, Indonesia, called Green School. The school is powered mainly from **renewable** energy sources that do not cause damage to Earth. Students at the school grow their own rice, fruit, and vegetables to serve in the school cafeteria.

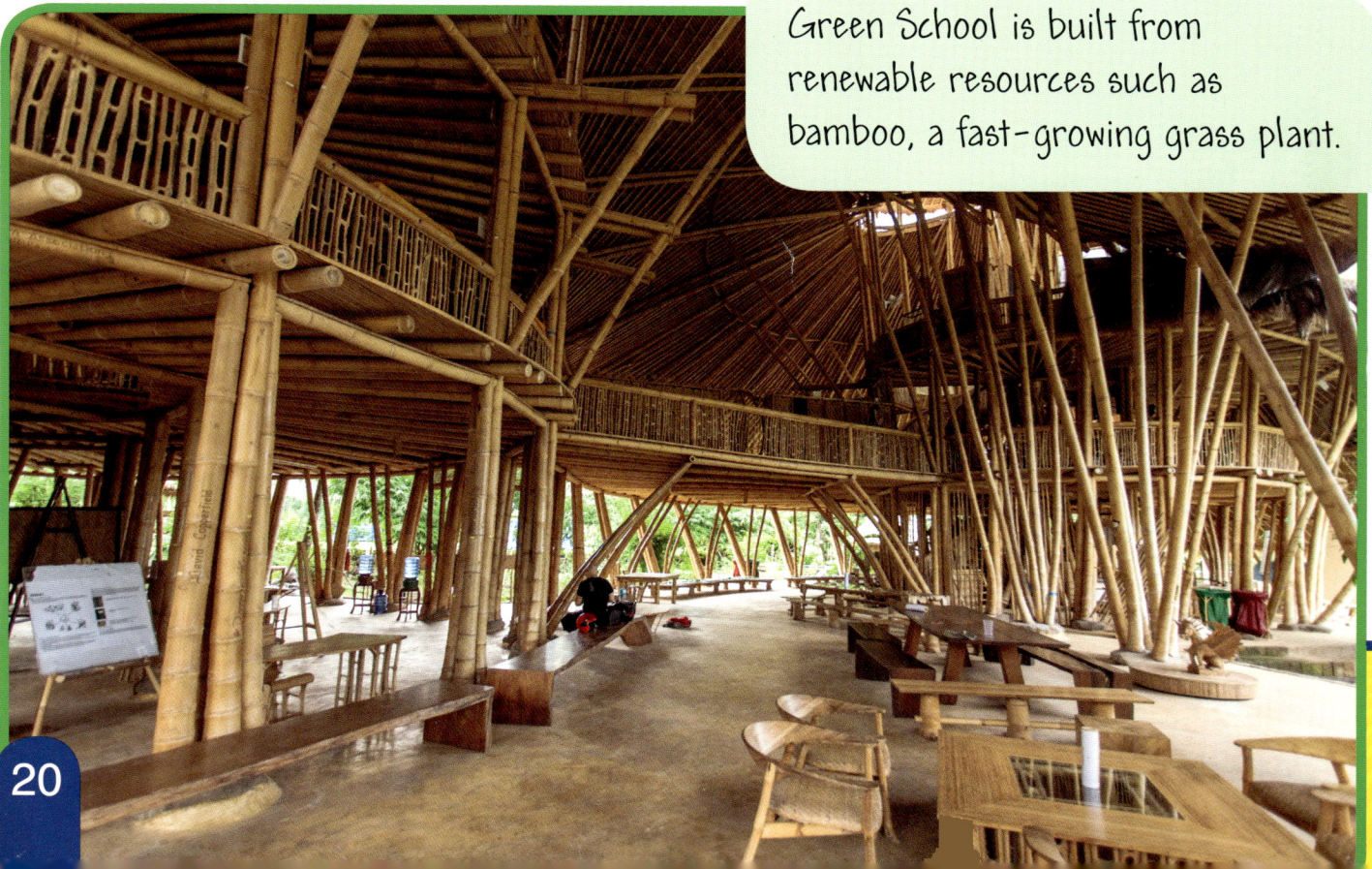

Green School is built from renewable resources such as bamboo, a fast-growing grass plant.

New schooling methods

Other schools are trying new methods of teaching children. The Brooklyn Free School in New York City, USA, lets students decide how they spend their school day. Students can choose between subjects like math and writing, or they can work on projects, such as starting a school newspaper. The school is not divided into grades, and no tests are given. The students even get to decide whether they attend classes.

Eighty students, from the ages of 4 to 18, can attend Brooklyn Free School each year .

Notes to Educators

Objective:

This title encourages readers to make global connections by understanding that even though children around the world go to different kinds of schools, all children who go to school learn similar skills and subjects.

Main Concepts Include:

- schools give children the opportunity to learn and meet people
- school buildings and daily structure may be different from one place to another, but most subject areas are the same

Discussion Prompts:

- Revisit the types of schools from around the world described in the book. Ask readers how they are the same and how they are different from the schools they attend. Have them create a Venn diagram to help with their comparisons.

Activity Suggestions:

- Invite children to think about the Brooklyn Free School model. How would they choose to spend their school day? Design what a typical school day would look like at their school.
- Encourage children to add as much detail as possible about their school day.
- Once completed, invite children to present their school plan.
- Guide students by providing questions for them to answer such as:
  - What subjects will be taught at your school?
  - How long will each school day be? How often will you go to school?
  - What rules will be followed at your school?
  - How will your school day be broken up? How much time will be spent in class on learning, playing, and eating?
- Encourage children to point out their favorite parts of the school day in the school they design.

Learning More

Books

A School Like Mine: A Unique Celebration of Schools Around the World.
DK Publishing, 2007.

Kalman, Bobbie. *My School Community*. Crabtree Publishing Company, 2010.

Welbourn, Shannon. *Be the Change in your School*.
Crabtree Publishing Company, 2014.

Websites

www.kidsdiscover.com/teacherresources/schools-around-the-world/
Learn about a typical school day for students in different countries.

www.cbc.ca/books/kids/OffToClass.pdf
Check out this e-book about unique types of schools around the world, and learn about other students in your global community!

www.greenschools.net
Take a quiz to see how green your school is. Get tips on how to make your school more environmentally friendly!

Glossary

Note: Some **boldfaced** words are defined where they appear in the book.

blackboard [BLAK-bawrd] (noun) A sheet of dark, hard material written on with chalk

environment [en-VAHY-ruh n-muh nt) (noun) Everything that surrounds us

Jewish [JOO-ish] (adjective) Relating to the religion of Judiasm and to its culture

Judaism [JOO-de-iz-uh m] (noun) The religion of the Jewish people who follow one God

Muslim [is-LAHM] (noun) A person that follows the religion of Islam

renewable [ri-NOO-uh-bul] (adjective) Able to be replaced, such as a tree

responsibility [ri-spon-suh-BIL-i-tee] (noun) Having a duty to do or complete something

rural [ROO R-uh l] (adjective) Having to do with the countryside.

shifts [shift s] (noun) A set period of time for work or other activities that is usually switched in turn with others

unique [yoo-NEEK] (adjective) Something that is unlike anything else; on its own

urban [UR-buh n] (adjective) Having to do with a city.

whiteboard [HWAHYT-bawrd] (noun) A sheet of white, shiny material written on with markers

A noun is a person, place, or thing. An adjective tells us what something is like.

Index